THE THREE DREAMS

Thalia Alexiou

Illustrations by Christina Chourma

Full Court Press
Englewood Cliffs, New Jersey

First Edition

Copyright © 2022 by Thalia Alexiou

All rights reserved. No part of this book may be reproduced or transmitted in any form or by any means electronic or mechanical, including by photocopying, by recording, or by any information storage and retrieval system, without the express permission of the author, except where permitted by law.
Published in the United States of America
by Full Court Press, 601 Palisade Avenue,
Englewood Cliffs, NJ 07632

fullcourtpress.com

ISBN 978-1-7353679-1-0

Library of Congress Control No. 2022909767

Interior and Cover Art by Christina Chourma

Art Enhancement by Dimitrios Koletsis

Editing and book design by Barry Sheinkopf

TO MY PRECIOUS GRANDDAUGHTER

whose dreams inspired this book

As I was cleaning out my desk one day, I found a notebook—the notebook of treasured stories I had taken of my granddaughter Cleo's dreams. I'd always encouraged her to discuss her night dreams with me. It allowed me to share many lessons with her. Some of her dreams have been scary, others philosophical, and still others truly magical. Each offers a message that we can all learn from. While reviewing my notes, I came across the words *The Future*. I am writing this now because of them, because the future belongs to those who believe in the beauty of their dreams. I want to tell you three of them.

THE GOLDEN DUST

CLEO WAS TURNING FIVE. I could not miss her birthday, so I traveled to Philadelphia early in the morning to visit her. It was still early when I arrived. Everybody was there, her *mama* and *baba* as well as her brother Nikolas. The sunlight was stretching to peek through the Pappas family's windows.

Cleo was trying to wake up, too. She seemed preoccupied, and not with her birthday celebration. Her mind was on her birthday-eve dream.

Cleo was a dreamer, and she often shared her midnight adventures with me. That day was no different. I was sitting at the kitchen table when she came to me. "Happy Birthday, Cleo!" I stretched my arms wide, enveloping her with birthday love.

She sat on my lap. "*Yiayia*, I want to talk to you about my dream. It was such a beautiful dream." Her eyes lit up as the sunlight swept golden hues throughout the room.

I grabbed her face and kissed her forehead. As she pulled away, I nodded. "Go ahead, honey."

Cleo sat down across the table from me and closed her eyes as if reliving her dream. She inhaled. "*Yiayia*, we were walking in the park when, all of a sudden, we started to *fly!*" She reached her arms out and teetered them through the air. "We were looking down into the park when we became surrounded by clouds. There was this one cloud. . . ." She drew the shape of a cloud over her head with her arched arms. "This cloud was shiny. Gold. Glittery. It came to us as we flew, so we went inside it." Her arms fluttered forward with

her hands sculpting the shape of the billowy tufts that surrounded her in her dream. "Then, *Yiayia*—" Cleo leaned toward me— "we looked around, and we could see that the cloud was shining like a golden sun. Golden dust was *everywhere!*" She shot her arms up into the air and looked around the room as if she were again surrounded by the golden dust. "The golden dust covered us, and then it began to fall onto the trees and people in the park."

Cleo placed her hands on the table and paused as she looked up at me, grimacing. "But I lost you." She bowed her head.

"That's okay," I said, having a hunch that we would reunite in her dream.

Cleo nodded. "I kept flying, and the golden dust was scattering on the roofs of all the buildings through the city. And then. . .then I *found you!*"

Her bright expression made me smile.

"You were in that special building, the one that looks like a castle." Cleo shifted her arms and eyes to the ceiling as if she were standing in front of the castle-like building. "And you wore a long, beautiful purple dress. It was covered with golden dust." She shifted towards me again. "You started flying again. And there were more and more people flying!"

Cleo and I started to sway from side to side as if maneuvering through the sky above the city. "And guess what?"

"What?" I asked.

"My friend Charlie was there! He was flying around New York City, too!"

That was the first time Cleo recognized that her dream had taken place in New York City. I asked her, "How do you know it was New York, darling?"

She was unfazed. "*Mama* and *Baba* took me there once. That was definitely New York City, and we flew and flew through the golden dust all night."

I moved to her side of the table, gave her a big hug, and sat next to her. "That was a beautiful dream, honey."

She agreed. "Do you think I'll get to fly surrounded by golden dust again?" she asked.

I paused. "Both in your dreams and in real life, you can believe that you are enshrouded with golden dust. It's *goodness*. Each night, before you go to bed, think about sending golden dust to all the children of the world."

"I will, *Yiayia*."

"It's a blessing to be grateful and to have beautiful thoughts. The more we send beautiful thoughts out into the world, the more beautiful the world we'll build. Don't you agree, Cleo?"

"*Okay, Yiayia!*"

THE APPLE TREES

ONE SATURDAY ON THE EVE of the Greek Independence Parade, I was again at my family's Philadelphia home to have a traditional Greek seafood dinner with her and her family. Cleo and Nikolas were thrilled to have their grandmother spend the night in their home.

The day of the parade, I awoke and prepared my coffee. As I was adjusting to the atmosphere in the cozy kitchen, I heard the pitter-patter of my granddaughter's feet on the wooden floors. Cleo soon appeared, scowling. I set down my coffee cup. "What happened, sweetie? Are you okay?"

Cleo shrugged her shoulders. "I had a bad dream, *Yiayia*." She lifted her head, her sad eyes peering into mine.

I reached out my arms. "Come here."

She shuffled into my embrace, and I gave her a big, comforting hug. "Honey, don't be sad. It's only a dream."

She shrugged again.

"Do you want to talk about it?"

Cleo nodded.

"Let's have a glass of milk first," I said, "and then you can tell me all about it." I went to the cupboard, then the refrigerator, and filled two glasses of milk—one for her, and one for me. I handed hers to her, and we headed to the living room to sit on the couch. She nestled towards me, carefully balancing her glass.

"I'm listening, my Cleo."

Her eyes sank in sorrow to the floor. "I was with Nikolas and *Mama*, and we were walking in Philadelphia. There were lots of trees." Cleo turned towards me, her eyes widening. "A *lot* of trees, *Yiayia*. It looked like a *forest*, in the middle of the city!"

"Oh!" I responded.

She grasped her glass with two hands. "The trees were running *after* us! They were *yelling* at us! They were throwing *rotten apples* at us! It was very, very scary, *Yiayia*." Cleo nestled closer.

"It's okay, Cleo. It's just a dream."

—13—

She took a deep breath. "We started running. We somehow realized that the apples the trees were throwing at us were poisonous. As we ran, the trees continued screaming at us. "Eat my poison apples!" they shouted. We started running faster, but Nikolas could not keep up. He lagged behind. I was getting scared. Luckily, *Mama*, like a superhero, grabbed him, and then we escaped."

Cleo let out a deep breath. "And then we were safe."

"And you are safe now," I assured her.

She nodded, taking a careful sip of milk. She turned to me and smiled. I smiled in return, and we both laughed. "Talking trees," she giggled. "What do you think it means, *Yiayia*?"

"Well, Cleo, maybe the trees were bad because we poison them with pollution and chemicals."

This was a real discovery for Cleo. "Ah!" she whispered.

"Keep that in mind, sweetie. Always eat organic fruits, and respect Mother Earth, and you will then have nothing to worry about."

Cleo nodded in agreement and looked up at me for more.

"You see, my darling, it was only a dream, so you are safe. But *because* it was a dream, it's important that we learn the message the dream is sending."

"Okay, *Yiayia*."

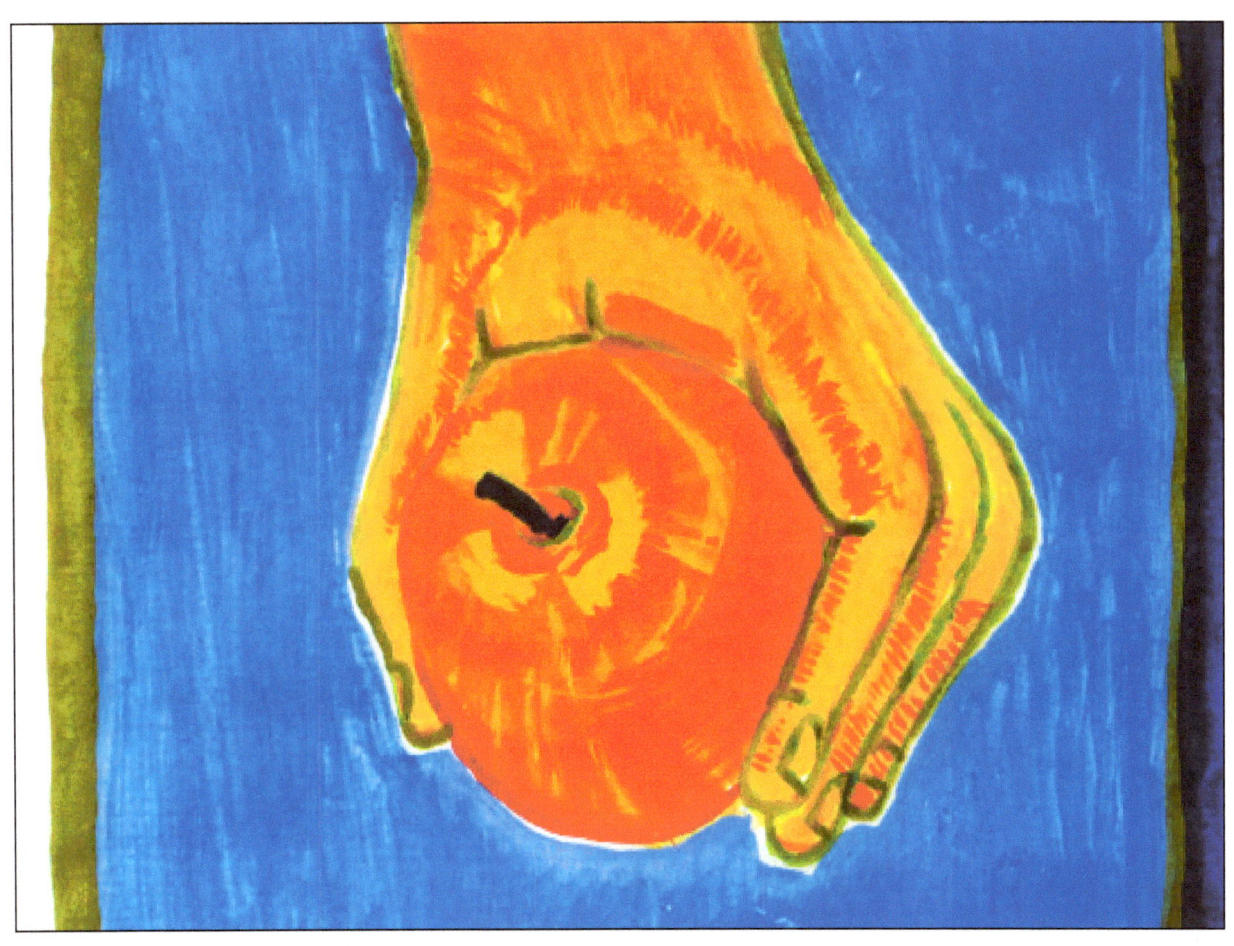

"We learn from everything around us. Now, let's get prepared for the parade."

Cleo shrieked in excitement. "Thank you for the beautiful message, *Yiayia*."

"Of course."

By that time, the rest of the family had assembled in the kitchen. The table was set, and a large stack of pancakes, with pure honey and cinnamon, was situated in the middle of it. We sat down, sharing our blessings. Before we ate, I exclaimed, "Thank you, God, for this blessed day!" It was the perfect morning for it. We were grateful for each other and the glorious lessons that life teaches us.

THE WITCH

I HAD JUST RETURNED FROM VACATION, so I headed to the Pappas' home to visit my daughter, her husband, and my grandkids. They were excited to see me, and I was thrilled to see them. I walked through the door to a cacophony of joyous shrieks and screams. "*Yiayia* is here!" The kids' enthusiasm echoed throughout the house.

They ran toward my outreached arms. "I have *missed* you!" I said.

"We have missed *you!*" they replied in unison.

After many kisses and hugs, I said, "Why don't we go out to dinner at your favorite place?"

The kids jumped up and down, grinning from ear to ear. "Oh, yes!" Cleo exclaimed. "I'm going to dress up in a dreamy dress, *Yiayia*. The one you bought for me." She twirled in the entryway before running off to her room.

I made my way into the living room, and before I knew it, she returned. She was wearing a fluffy purple dress. She *looked* like a fairy. Her enthusiasm encouraged us all to ready ourselves and head out to a local spot that serves delicious Mediterranean food.

We sat around the table. I was happily sandwiched between the kids. We spent our time talking about my vacation and what the kids had done when I was gone. The food arrived, and the adults enjoyed the very fresh grilled fish and salad. The kids loved what they had chosen, too: grilled cheese, a Cyprus favorite.

When we were done eating, Cleo leaned over and whispered in

my ear, "*Yiayia*, I had a dream when you were gone."

I leaned back in my chair. "Do you remember it?"

Cleo nodded. "Yes, I do."

"Well, when we get home, I promise to listen to your dream."

"Okay, *Yiayia*!"

We finished our dinner and the delightful conversation that accompanied it, and headed home. Remembering my promise, as we walked in the door of the Pappas home, I turned to Cleo. "I will make a fresh cup of coffee, and then I will be all ears to hear your dream, sweetie."

She nodded.

I headed to the kitchen. Cleo headed to her room to put on her cozy, dream-telling pajamas. She returned just as I was pouring a fresh cup of coffee. We met at the couch and sank onto the cushions. She cozied up beside me.

"So, my sweetie, tell me your dream. I can't wait to hear about it."

Cleo looked at the door. "In my dream, *Yiayia*, a witch had knocked on our door, and *Baba* opened it." Cleo turned back to me and screeched, "Out of the blue, the witch grabbed him, pushed him on the floor, and started jumping on him." She shook her head. "*Baba* was screaming, 'Help, help, help!'" Cleo was more excited than scared as she bounced up and down. "I called *Mama* for help, but she didn't come. So I grabbed the witch by her long hair." Cleo grasped the air as if holding onto the witch's locks. "And then I pulled her towards the door and *threw her out!*" Cleo dredged her hands together. A job well done. She continued, "*Baba* thanked me and said, 'Cleo, I did not know you were that strong. You are even stronger than me! Thank you again!'"

Cleo grinned. "I told him, 'You're welcome, *Baba!*'"

"I see," I said. "You are strong. You know what else?"

Cleo anticipated the lesson I was to share. "That dream was not about hurting others."

Cleo looked at me quizzically.

"The witch was *scared* of *Baba*," I said, "and maybe she thought that Baba was going to hurt *her*. *That's* why she acted that way."

Cleo let out a long "Hmmm," absorbing the lesson.

I continued, "The word 'witch' means 'wise woman.' In the dream, maybe she was a wise person who could fly and heal. Something else about witches—they have a great deal of knowledge about herbs and all living things on Earth." But people are afraid of them because not everyone has that kind of knowledge."

Cleo gazed at me intently.

"People have been attacking witches because they think witches are bad. As a result, the witches must protect themselves, so they don't get hurt. That's why they attack first. That's why the witch attacked *Baba*. *Baba* wasn't going to hurt her, but she didn't know this. She acted out of fear. By you helping *Baba*, you showed how brave you are, and I am so proud of you."

Cleo smiled and turned to face me. "*Yiayia*, can you read to me, please?"

It was such a beautiful return visit with the family. I was so grateful to be in their lives and to have them. "Of course, Cleo, I will read to you."

ACKNOWLEDGMENTS

For help with the writing of this story, I want to thank Litsa Psaraftis, Michael Kokkinakis, Sotiris Zafeiris, Anna Spyrou, and Theodora Lecour.

I'd also like to thank my grandparents, Nikolas Hadjipetrou and Sevasti Tampoura, who always believed in my dreams. My grandfather used to say, "We are all equal." My grandmother taught me a way to analyze my dreams. My father always shared his stories and taught me how to tell my own. I am grateful as well to my mother and my siblings. And I am thankful for lifelong friends Louiza Bratsou, Dr. Helene Leonetti, Dr. Michael Kokkinaris, Barbara Di Marco, and Ana Di Marco, who have believed in me. They always believed in me.

Finally, God bless my beloved husband, Dr. Kriss Stavrinos, who unfailingly supports all my wild dreams.

How To Use This Book

1. Read it with your child.

2. Interpret wisdom in your own way.

3. Point out gratitude.

4. Explain blessings.

5. Analyze acts of kindness.

6. Clarify happiness.

7. Describe why it is important not to hurt others.

8. Illustrate both sides of the coin.

9. Keep dreaming big!